I0475996

How To Work With An ASSHOLE

(productively)

Help on how to get by with your sanity still intact
when working with the less-than perfect.

Jack Dayton and Torin Blackhawk

DEDICATION

To all those who have suffered.
To all those who don't have to.

CONTENTS

ACKNOWLEDGMENTS

We would like to acknowledge you, you asshole, for all you've taught us; for all we've put in this book. To you, we say thank you—you asshole.

1 HELLO

Hi. Never thought you'd see the day when you'd pick up a book like this one huh?

Well, that's okay. Neither did we. But it happens to us all…apparently. Maybe we can give you a little advice through this small book, and make your life a little easier.

If anything, maybe we can change your state and get a laugh out of you. At least then, you'll feel better.

So, if you still feel the need to learn how to work with an asshole, read on…

We've made some assumptions in this book, like, you are in the lower position; unable to change or fire "them" through the system, or otherwise.

2 YOU VS. THEM

Or should I say just them…and you get whatever is left over. No, it's not quite that bad, but some people may think so…

Be Yourself (mostly).

You'll kill yourself if you're not yourself. That's pretty simple, but easy to overlook when your new and just trying to learn things.

Do it in a mellow way. Yes, be yourself, but don't brag about it to everyone—especially anyone who might be an asshole.

You, subdued, is a good way to think of how to go about your life at your current employment.

If you want a change, you need to be the change (cause they ain't). This old cliché is true. If you see something not working, then YOU have to do something about it.

They're NOT changing. Period. They may give it lip service, but that's it.

Especially if they've got seniority. A lot of assholes love this—and will tell you about it any way they can.

Especially if they're OLD. It must be like a built-in seniority, even if they have less experience than you. But watch out for those old seniority types. The worst...

They've "done it all". Yeah, and you'll never win an argument again. So don't even try. (I'm trying to save you a few years of your life here.)

"It Ain't About You". And it never will be either.

When you're new, you "just don't know how it is around here." But even when you have been "here" for years, they'll still think you don't know crap. Odd how that happens.

3 LEARNING

Think you were done learning when you got out of school? Sorry. Better pack it up again and get ready to take notes like you never have before.

Learn Them. All of them. Every last detail you can, short of becoming a stalker at work.

Their speech. Know it when you hear it. Even at crowed stadium 50 feet away.

Their body language. Read the minutia. This will tell you 90% or more of what they really mean.

Their work habits. If for no other reason than to know when the bathroom is clear. OMG...

Their personal history; if they share that with you. Don't ask. Never ask. But if you get, treat it like gold. It will be a valuable asset when you least expect it.

Then DON'T forget it! EVER!

Learn From Them.

Just listen. I can't put it any other way.

They may be REALLY good at something, so you can learn it from them (if you want to). If you feel like you may have a need to know how to turn a chain into a knife at some point in your life, then pay attention. You actually will learn something. But in general, you may be able to advance beyond them by learning from them. Unless of course your employer is smaller than an ice-cream cone stand.

ASK them to teach you—anything. It will give you a fallback when you need something to talk about while on break, waiting for a meeting to start, or the 5:00 whistle to blow.

On Talking With Them

LISTEN.

FOCUS on the subject THEY brought up; and nothing more.

Follow up on their issues—every time!

Keep on work only—forget making a personal bond. There is no need to ask about their kid(s). You're nobody they want around them anyway (even if they are older than you).

You may ask questions, but keep your comments to yourself (they don't care what you think anyway). And please, just stick to the questions.

4 ACTING

No, we're not talking like Tom Cruise, or Shakespeare; but it could land you a promotion instead of a Grammy!

Act Like A Moron—"Yes Boss." Sounds dumb and stupid, but it's gotten me through a lot of crap I didn't want to have to deal with in any other manner.

Don't question them. Pretend they are really omniscient. Even if they don't even know what the word means.

But do know your boundaries. Don't act too much. There is a limit, but I can't define yours for you. I just hope there's some invisible fence that shocks you before you go too far.

Take all the work you get, and like it (don't judge it). Then you can maybe stay busy and out of the way!

Don't Be Ambitious. Especially if you're in a dead-end job.

Put their needs first. And maybe even tell them so—it will boost their thoughts of you (but only a teeny-weeny bit).

Act as a supporter, or cheerleader. Let them know when they've done good; even if for no other reason than this is a good life skill to have.

Ask how you can help, not for their help. They don't have time for you, but you should always make time for them.

Do Small Things For Them.

Send the reminder emails. To them, to their boss (and cc them!), and customers (if you have any).

Clean-up. The floor. The room. The mess. The _____. You're now the janitor (congratulations!).

Let them go home early, and you finish up. After all, you wanted the comp time didn't you?

Keep It Inside

Your emotions.

Your thoughts.

Stay calm and happy yourself—inside

Don't outwardly express emotion. It is not
worth it. I don' know how to get this one across,
but if you miss it, you will never forget it.

5 SEPARATING

Yeah, when all else fails, sometimes you just have to say bye-bye.

Stay away. Stay away.   Stay away.

Work on your own every chance you get.

Help others—and stay away all you can.

Call in sick, if you need time NOW. DO NOT overestimate the power of sick time!

Go on Vacation—take 6 weeks or more and write a book like this—just like I am. It feels good to let off steam!

L E A V E

Don't let it get as bad as we have it now. I mean had ☺.

When all else fails, walking away will leave you with a chance to start fresh and know what to look out for next time.

*When you get a better offer—from anyone, or anyplace!

*You can't stand it anymore. Your call—always will be.

*If/when you can move departments—options I wish I had.

*You get the promotion—TAKE IT!

(Way to go champ! You passed Asshole 101—now you're on to Advanced Assholes!)

6 GOOD LUCK

Well, I hope this has been fun, educational, and eye-opening for you. We've done what we felt was our "civic" duty ; that of informing others of the horrors that await them if they don't pay attention to workplace issues, troubles and assholes.

If you laughed at any of this, then maybe you still have a chance. Just remember—don't get caught by the asshole, while doodling the asshole, and you'll be fine!

ABOUT THE AUTHORS

Jack Dayton was formerly working for a dumbass who left him under the assault of an asshole. He is now currently working for himself as a consultant…and teaching others that there is a better way than working with an asshole.

Torin Blackhawk also worked with Jack Dayton under the same dumbass and same asshole. For her, the experience was beyond description, so she decided to put most of her emotions into doodles (so there'll be a second edition to share them!). She is now pursuing a higher degree…and is prepared to handle any future asshole.

www.ingramcontent.com/pod-product-compliance
Lightning Source LLC
Chambersburg PA
CBHW051422170526
45165CB00004BA/1924